THE LITTLE JUGGLER

THE
LITTLE JUGGLER

Adapted from
an Old French Legend
and Illustrated

by

Barbara Cooney

HASTINGS HOUSE, PUBLISHERS, NEW YORK

For Barnaby

Juv
cop 3

5

A WORD ABOUT THIS BOOK

Fifteen years ago at Christmastime I heard on the radio the story of the little juggler of Notre Dame. Well-known to many people, this ancient legend was then new to me. I was charmed. The story was so simple and so lovely. I decided to name my next child, if it were a boy, after the little juggler. It was and I did. I also decided that I would try to convince a publisher to publish again this old story and let me illustrate it. This has happened too. Since I first heard it, I have searched in many places for a version of the story that would suit my purposes. The legend has been written often and in many ways. The oldest version known is a seven hundred-year-old manuscript written in Old French, now carefully preserved in the *Bibliothèque de l'Arsenal* in Paris. About ninety years ago this manuscript was brought to public attention. Anatole France used it as the basis of a short story. Massenet turned it into an opera. There are a good many recent versions, including a delightful one for children printed not long ago in Chile.

In my book I am presenting a new adaptation of the old legend. I have added a few things; I have taken away others. But the story is basically the same.

Recently I have been to France to find and draw places where the little juggler might have wandered. I have returned with many pictures, many ideas, and photographs of the fragile old manuscript in Paris. I hope that I will do justice to this lovely legend. It will be my contribution to Christmas, 1961.

BARBARA COONEY,
Pepperell, Massachusetts

NCE UPON A TIME,
many more than a hundred years ago, there
lived a certain minstrel boy, a boy named
Barnaby, whose tale I now will tell you
even as it was told to me. He had neither
mother nor father, no, not even a roof to
call his own. He wandered far, to and fro,
and in many places. Like a snail, he carried
on his back all that he had in the world,
for he owned only the clothes he wore and
a few articles rolled inside a worn rug
which he carried on his shoulders. These
things inside his rug were his treasures:
two sticks, a few hoops, some balls, and a
handful of apples. For he was a street juggler, nothing more nor less.

7

Barnaby earned his bread by juggling
and tumbling, dancing and singing. How
to leap and spring, to juggle and balance
objects in mid-air, these things he knew
well, but nothing much besides. He knew
nothing of books—in fact, he knew only
what his father had taught him, for his
father had been a juggler also.

Now, Barnaby's mother had died when
he was a baby, but his father lived until
the spring when Barnaby became ten. Until then they travelled the land together,
amusing the people both high and low, in
the market squares and at the fairs, at
weddings and on feast days. For this the
people tossed them coppers, and with these
coins they bought their bread.

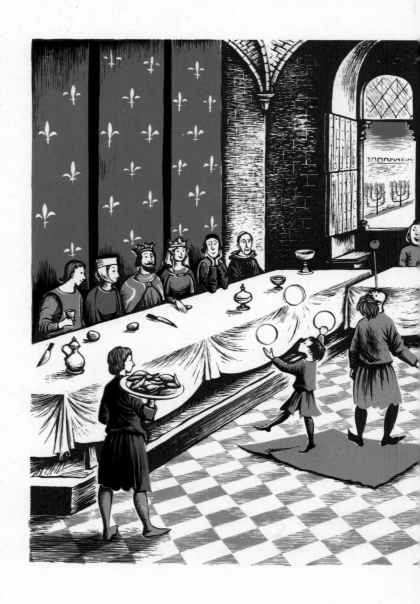

Now and
again they had the good fortune to entertain the lords and ladies at some great feast
within a castle. Then their pockets jingled
with silver, and they sat gratefully in a
dark corner of the great hall after they had
finished their tricks, munching the leftover
meat and pastries with the dogs.

After his father died, Barnaby was alone.
In order to eat he did as he had been taught,
for it was all that he knew. He spread his
shabby rug in the squares on market day
and leaped and danced and juggled with
all his might.

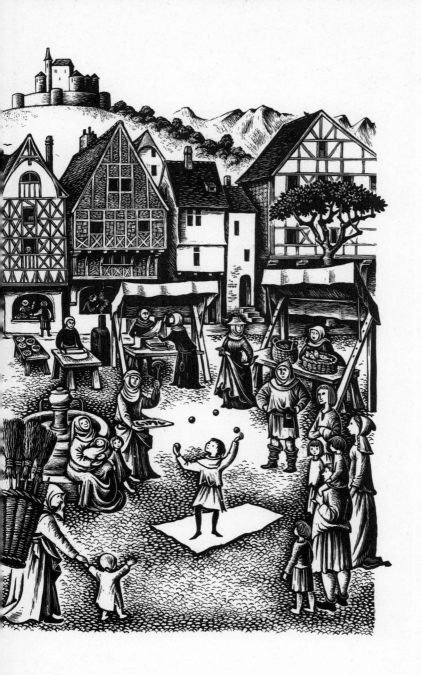

He appeared at inns to entertain the
guests.

He even found his way across draw-
bridges and through strong gates of castles
where he solemnly begged to be allowed
to entertain the lord and his lady.

If the people laughed when first they saw the small clown, they ended by showering coins on his rug when his tricks were over, for Barnaby had been well taught indeed. Young as he was, all went well, or as best it could, the rest of that spring and through the months of summer as he trudged across the countryside. The sky was his roof and the weather and the people were kind to him.

But when the chill of
winter began to creep into the houses and
into the bones of men, fewer and fewer
people stood still in the cold long enough
to watch Barnaby at his tricks in the market place. In the castles the lords and ladies
wore their fur-lined mantles. In the mon-

asteries the monks wore garments of lambs'
wool as they prayed in their cold churches.
In the cottages the peasants put on all the
clothes they owned.

And Barnaby, despite the exercise of
tumbling and juggling, shivered. The
coppers he picked up were few indeed.

22

One day, frozen and forlorn, he stood on his mat and bowed. Snowflakes had started to fall. One person only watched the boy, a monk who had come to the market from a nearby abbey to buy provisions for the kitchen. When Barnaby had finished, the monk spoke to the boy, saying, "Where is your home?"

Barnaby looked at the ground and shook his head, saying nothing for fear that words would bring his tears.

"Come," said the monk, "come with me.
You can warm yourself in our kitchen."
Barnaby did so. The abbey became his
home.

27

But at first the little tumbler, for all the
good fortune of having a roof over his head
and decent clothes on his back and enough
food to eat, moved among the monks sad
and ashamed. He saw the monks about
him, each serving God in his appointed
way. Whenever he went, upstairs and
down, in every quiet corner, in office and
cloister, he saw the monks at work and
prayer.

"Woe is me," he said. "O wretched me,
what am I doing here? All the rest are
serving God but me. I have no business
here. I know not even how to pray aright
and do naught but eat the bread they give
me."

Barnaby grew yet sadder as Christmas approached, for all about him everyone worked harder still. On Christmas Eve in the little chapel the monks would present to the Christ Child and His Mother the things that they had been making for them during the long year. One monk was writing a song. Another was penning the words to it. Still another was painstakingly copying a book of hours. Others were ornamenting its pages with flowers and scenes from the life of the Virgin Mary. Several monks together were carving a beautiful altar screen of oak for the little chapel that contained the statue of Our Lady and the Christ Child.

One day Barnaby knelt before the statue. "Holy Mary," he prayed, "how can I serve you?" Then in despair he wept. He hung his head and wished he had never been born. When he heard the bells ring for Mass, an idea entered his head. He sprang to his feet. "Shall I do it? Yes, I can and I will. I will do that which I have learned and thus, after mine own manner, I will serve the Christ Child and His Mother in her chapel. The others may honour them with songs and chants. I will serve with tumbling."

While the monks filed into the great church for Mass, Barnaby ran and fetched his rug and his sticks, his hoops, his balls and his apples. Hurrying back to the little chapel, he removed his robe. He laid his shabby rug before the altar and stood before Mary and the Child in his tunic, so thin that it was little better than a shift.

"Sweet Lady," said he, "to your protection I give myself. Scorn not the only thing I know, for with the help of God I will try to serve in the only way I can. How to chant or how to read to you I

know not. All I can do is set before you
my best tricks. I shall be like the bull calf
that leaps and bounds before its mother.
Whatever I am I shall be for you."

He began to turn somersaults, now high, now low, first forward, then backward. Then he started to juggle his hoops and then his apples, and then his hoops and apples together, all the time balancing a stick on the tip of his nose. Then, as the chants of the monks rose louder from the church, he tumbled and leaped and turned gaily his somersaults and walked on his two hands, all the while juggling his rings and apples until he fell exhausted at the feet of the statue. Finally, with a humble heart, he raised his face.

"Sweet Lady," he said, "this I do for you and for your Son. I can do no more." Then he sighed, for he knew not how else to pray. "The others chant your praises in the church but I will return each day to this chapel to entertain you with my tricks."

Still looking at the image, he dressed himself and went his way.

In this manner many days passed. Barnaby went each day into the little chapel. Never was he too tired to do his best to entertain the Mother and the Child.

Now, of course, the brothers knew that the boy went every day to the little chapel, but no one knew, save God, what he did there. Nor did he wish that any of his goings and doings should be seen, for he believed that were his secret once discovered he would be chased from the cloister and sent back again to the cold world.

The time came when Christmas was but two days away. On that very day one of the monks who had noticed Barnaby's absence from Mass decided to keep watch on him. So he watched and spied and followed until he saw the boy plying his trade in the little chapel.

"By my faith," whispered the monk to himself, "here is fine sport! Methinks that the sins of all the rest of us put together cannot equal this. While the others are at prayer and work, this tumbler dances proudly in the chapel. Thus he repays us. We chant for him and he tumbles for us!

Would that the brothers could see him
with their very own eyes, as I do this mo-
ment. Not a soul, methinks, could keep
from laughing at the sight of this little fool
killing himself with somersaults."

With these words he went at once to the
Abbot and told him all from beginning to
end. Whereon the Abbot rose to his feet
and said to the monk: "Now, I bid you
hold your peace and do not tell this tale
against your little brother. The next time
he goes to the chapel we will go together.
I would not have the boy blamed since he
knows no better."

The next night, on Christmas Eve, the
monks came to the little chapel with the
beautiful gifts for the Christ Child and His
Mother. Barnaby, with sad heart, watched
as each of the brothers laid his offering at
the feet of the statue.

"Ah, sweet Lady," he sighed, "if only I
could match the splendour of their gifts.
Alas, I cannot."

When the service was over and the monks had returned to their cells, Barnaby crept back to the chapel, unnoticed by all save the spying monk and the Abbot. These two went quietly and hid themselves hard by the altar in a nook where he could not see them. Barnaby bowed to the statue and laid aside his robe. The monk and the Abbot saw his somersaults, his merry leaping and dancing, how he capered and juggled and walked on his two hands before the image until he was near fainting. This night, the birthday of the Christ Child, Barnaby worked harder and with greater skill than he had ever done before. When he had done, so weary was he, that he sank to the ground. There he lay all worn out.

Suddenly, while the Abbot and the prying monk looked, they saw descend from the statue's niche a Dame more glorious than any man had ever seen before, richly crowned and beautiful. Her garments were shining with gold and precious stones. Around her were the angels from heaven above. They drew close about the little boy. The Lady Mary took a white napkin and fanned her tumbler with it. Gently she fanned his neck and face and body and gave herself to the care of him. Then she returned to the niche above, but before she went she bent and kissed her little juggler.

Then was the spying monk filled with shame. His confusion made him glow like fire.

"Mercy, Sire. I have judged the boy wrongly. He is indeed a saint."

Barnaby heard not their whispers. Having finished his tricks, he dressed himself and joyfully went his way.

And so it came to pass that on the day after Christmas the Abbot sent for Barnaby, and the boy was greatly troubled.

"Alas, I am found out. Ah, me, what shall I do? What shall I say? I do naught that is right. Woe is me. Surely they will bid me be gone."

He came before the Abbot with tears still wet on his cheeks and knelt upon the ground.

"Will you send me from your door, Sire? Tell me what you would have me do, and I shall do it."

Then replied the Abbot: "Answer me truly. Many weeks have you lived here. What service have you given and how have you earned your bread?"

"Sire," said the boy, "well knew I that
I should be sent upon my way as soon as
my doings were known. Now I will go.
Miserable am I, and miserable shall I be,
for I do naught to deserve my bread."

Then the Abbot raised him and kissed
his two eyes.

"Little brother," said he, "hold now your
peace, for I promise you that you shall stay
here always. You and I will be true friends.
And now, dear brother, I command you to
do this service—just as you did before—
but openly and as well as you know how."

"Sire, is this truly so?"

"Yes," said the Abbot, "yes, truly."

So, very cheerfully and with still greater skill, did Barnaby continue to ply his craft for the Christ Child and His Mother. Cheerfully did he tumble and cheerfully did he serve.

Here endeth the story of the little juggler of Our Lady.